Women in Profile

Visual & Performing Artists

Shaun Hunter

Crabtree Publishing Company

Dedication

This series is dedicated to every woman who has followed her dreams and to every young girl who hopes to do the same. While overcoming great odds and often oppression, the remarkable women in this series have triumphed in their fields. Their dedication, hard work, and excellence can serve as an inspiration to all—young and old, male and female. Women in Profile *is both an acknowledgment of and a tribute to these great women.*

Project Coordinator
Leslie Strudwick
Crabtree Editor
Virginia Mainprize
Editing and Proofreading
Carlotta Lemieux
Alana Luft
Krista McLuskey
Design
Warren Clark

Published by Crabtree Publishing Company

350 Fifth Avenue, Suite 3308
New York, NY
USA 10018

360 York Road, R.R. 4
Niagara-on-the-Lake
Ontario, Canada
L0S 1J0

Copyright © 1999 WEIGL EDUCATIONAL PUBLISHERS LIMITED. All rights reserved. No part of this publication may be reproduced, stored in a retrieval system, or transmitted in any form or by any means, electronic, mechanical, photocopying, recording, or otherwise, without the prior written permission of Weigl Educational Publishers Limited.

Cataloging-in-Publication Data

Hunter, Shaun, 1961–
    Visual & performing artists / Shaun Hunter.
        p. cm. — (Women in profile)
    Includes bibliographical references and index.
    Summary: Chronicles the lives and achievements of talented women in the arts, including painter Georgia O'Keeffe, dancer Natalia Makarova, singer Buffy Sainte-Marie, and comedian Lily Tomlin.
    ISBN 0-7787-0035-6 (pbk) — ISBN 0-7787-0013-5 (rlb)
    1. Women artists—Biography—Juvenile literature. [1. Artists. 2. Women—Biography.] I. Title. II. Series.
NX90.H86   1999
700'.92'2—ddc21
[B]   98-39282
                                        CIP
                                        AC

Photograph Credits
Every reasonable effort has been made to trace ownership and to obtain permission to reprint copyright material. The publishers would be pleased to have any errors or omissions brought to their attention so that they may be corrected in subsequent printings.

Agence France Presse/Corbis-Bettmann: page 22; Archive Photos: cover, pages 14, 17, 20, 23, 24, 28, 30, 36, 45; Corbis-Bettmann: pages 12, 33; Image Works: pages 7, 8, 11, 29, 44; Photograph by Guillermo Kahlo: page 13; Northwestern State University of Louisiana, Watson Memorial Library, Cammie G. Henry Research Center: page 43; Photofest: pages 6, 18, 21, 26, 35, 42; Pictorial Press: page 19; Courtesy Buffy Sainte-Marie: pages 37, 38, 39, 40, 41; Topham Picture Point: 32 (Alfred Stieglitz); UPI/Corbis-Bettmann: pages 9, 10, 15,16, 27, 31, 34.

Contents

More Women in Profile

Visual & Performing Artists

Often, when you watch talented actors, singers, or dancers perform, their work seems effortless. They speak their lines naturally, sing easily, or move smoothly. When you look at a professional artist's painting, all the elements of the picture fit together. What you do not see in the performance or the painting are the many years of training and trial-and-error. For most artists, success comes only after a long **apprenticeship**, persistence, hard work, and a lucky break or two.

If you could name all the women performers and visual artists in the world, your list would be very long. This book focuses on the lives of only a handful of the hundreds of exceptional women performers and visual artists of the twentieth century. Each of the six major profiles follows one woman's journey as an artist. The stories show how each woman has used her creativity and worked hard to develop her skills. Each profile details some of the obstacles these women have encountered and explores their accomplishments, as artists and as individuals.

The last section of the book provides brief descriptions of several other women performers and visual artists you may wish to learn more about on your own.

Each of the artists in this book has taken a different career path. Some found an appreciative audience sooner than others did. Some lost favor with their audience for a time. Some paid no attention to what other people thought. All of these women, however, devoted themselves and their lives to their art.

Perhaps the stories of these talented women and their interesting lives will inspire you to learn about other women performers and visual artists. Perhaps, like the women in this book, you will pursue your own artistic journey.

"The singing never comes naturally.... I don't just get up and sing like a lark every morning. My voice sounds like a terrible rusty engine most mornings. And then I work it gradually. I have to warm up before going on stage, just as a dancer does."

Julie Andrews

British Singer and Actor

Early Years

As a child, Julie Wells was surrounded by music and dance. Her mother was a talented pianist, and her aunt ran a dancing school in their town just south of London, England. When she was just a toddler, Julie started taking tap and ballet lessons with her aunt. When she was three years old, Julie sang in the dancing school's musical play.

Julie's parents divorced when she was four years old. Her mother married the singer Ted Andrews, and they toured their **vaudeville** act throughout England. Julie often sang with them, standing on a wooden crate to reach the microphone. Julie's last name was eventually changed to Andrews, and the act was billed as The Andrews Family.

Julie was an amazing singer. As a young child, she could sing the same range of notes as an adult singer. Her stepfather urged her to begin serious voice training. Soon, she started taking lessons with a world-famous concert singer and teacher. Julie traveled alone by train each week to Leeds, a city 200 miles (320 kilometers) away. She spent four days a week with her teacher, taking two lessons a day.

BACKGROUNDER

Vaudeville Theater

Vaudeville shows were very popular in the music halls of England and the United States in the first few **decades** of the 1900s. A vaudeville show usually included performances by comedians, singers, dancers, and magicians. In The Andrews Family act, Julie sang **duets** with her stepfather while her mother played piano. As radio and movies became more widespread, live vaudeville shows became less popular and finally died out altogether.

Julie at home learning her lines for the play Mountain Fire.

Developing Skills

Julie's life was different from most children her age. She did not go to school but was tutored at home. She spent most of her days with adults, at singing lessons, or at the theaters where she performed with her mother and stepfather.

When Julie was twelve, she joined the cast of a musical **revue** in London's theater district. She became an overnight star. Soon, she was performing in musical productions all over England. She was so well paid that she began to support her family financially.

On stage, Julie was bubbly and outgoing. Off stage, she was a shy, private person. She loved spending time with her younger brothers at the Andrews home in the English countryside. When she was eighteen, she was asked to perform in the New York cast of a successful English musical, *The Boy Friend*. At first, she hesitated. Julie did not want to be so far away from her family for such a long time. She finally agreed to take one of the lead roles for one year.

Julie traveled all over England performing in musical revues.

In New York City, Julie had to work hard. Her role included many singing numbers and a great deal of acting. At first, Julie felt nervous because she had never trained as an actor. When *The Boy Friend* opened, it was a box-office hit. Julie was named one of the most promising new theater personalities and was given an award for an outstanding Broadway **debut**. After *The Boy Friend*, Julie's Broadway career took off quickly. She was offered leading roles in major musicals and decided to stay in the United States.

In spite of her growing popularity and success, Julie worried about each new role. She remembers feeling "an enormous weight every night. I can't remember a single performance when I didn't wonder to myself: 'Am I going to get through it tonight?'" During her years in New York, Julie continued to miss her family and her home in England.

BACKGROUNDER
Julie on Broadway

The late 1950s and early 1960s was a golden age for musical theater on Broadway, the theater district of New York City. Theater-goers could buy tickets to several star-studded Broadway productions including *Peter Pan*, *West Side Story*, *The Music Man,* and *Gypsy*. Between 1956 and 1962, Julie played two of the best-known female roles on Broadway. In the musical *My Fair Lady* she was the flower girl, Eliza Doolittle. In *Camelot*, she starred as Queen Guinevere.

"In the early days, performing was all I knew. It was my whole identity, and I used it for both gratification and to avoid a lot of soul searching."

Julie starred with Rex Harrison in the stage musical My Fair Lady.

Quick Notes

- In her career, Julie has made more than thirty-five recordings.

- For her performance in *Mary Poppins*, Julie earned an Academy Award for Best Actress.

- In 1965, Julie made her solo television debut. Thirty-five million viewers tuned into *The Julie Andrews Show*. She won two Emmy awards and a Peabody award for her performance.

- Julie was active in Operation California, now known as Operation America. This agency sends food, medicine, and other help to people around the world who are coping with disaster.

Accomplishments

In 1962, Julie was performing in the musical *Camelot*. During a matinee performance, Walt Disney was in the audience. Backstage after the show, he asked if Julie wanted to play the character of an English nanny in his new film *Mary Poppins*. When she accepted, Julie moved to Los Angeles with her husband and their infant daughter, Emma.

Released in the summer of 1964, *Mary Poppins* was an instant success. Julie became one of the most popular stars in the world. In the next three years, each of her six films was a hit. For a decade, Julie was one of the most successful and best-paid performers in the film business.

In the late 1960s, Julie's film success began to slow down. She continued making movies, but many were not successful. Julie was experimenting with more serious roles that did not reflect the image the public loved so well. Her fans and the press seemed to turn against her.

Mary Poppins launched Julie's film career. She won an Academy Award for her performance.

With her second husband, Blake Edwards, a Hollywood writer and director, Julie started a new family. She devoted herself to raising her daughter and her two stepchildren. Later, she and Blake adopted two infant Vietnamese girls, orphaned during the Vietnam War. The Edwards family left the pressures of Hollywood and for several years lived in Switzerland.

Julie continued her career as a recording artist and appeared in many television productions. In 1993, she returned to the New York stage. It had been thirty years since her last appearance on Broadway in *Camelot*. In 1995, she and Blake opened a stage version of their hit film, the musical *Victor/Victoria*. Julie recalls being "scared to death" before the opening of the show. For two years, she followed an exhausting schedule, performing eight shows a week.

With the success of *Victor/Victoria* behind her, Julie is considering new challenges in her career. Now in her sixties, she says, "I'm dying to explore and experiment."

BACKGROUNDER
Julie Edwards, Author

In 1971, Julie wrote her first children's book, *Mandy*, under her married name, Julie Edwards. Her stepdaughter, Jennifer, asked her to write the story. *Mandy* is about an orphan girl who desperately wants a family. Julie also wrote *The Last of the Really Great Wangdoodles* about a humorous monster. In 1996, Julie had these two stories published as *The Julie Andrews Edwards Treasury: Two Magical Novels*. Julie has also been working on a third book for children about a ship's cat.

"Earlier on, I would perform in order to run away from myself and from my life. But these days, I really run to embrace it."

One of Julie's most famous roles was Maria in **The Sound of Music.** *This movie broke box office records around the world.*

"The only thing I know is that I paint because I need to, and I paint always whatever passes through my head, without any other consideration."

Frida Kahlo

Mexican Artist

Early Years

Frida Kahlo was born in a village not far from Mexico City. She and her three sisters grew up in the bright blue house her father had built. Frida's father was a professional photographer and an amateur painter. He shared his love of art and nature with Frida.

Frida was a free-spirited girl. At school, she often got into trouble. When she was six, Frida contracted **polio**. The polio made her right leg weak and smaller than her left leg. When the other children teased her, Frida found comfort in an imaginary friend. Despite her weak leg, she took up soccer, boxing, swimming, and cycling.

When she was fourteen, Frida started classes at one of the best schools in Mexico. She was one of the few girls at the school. She planned to be a doctor. When Frida was eighteen, the wooden bus in which she was riding home from school was rammed by a streetcar. Frida suffered so many injuries that her doctors did not think she would survive. She was so determined to live that after a month she returned home from the hospital.

BACKGROUNDER

Casa Azul

The stucco walls of Frida's home were painted bright blue. Everyone called it the Casa Azul (Spanish for blue house). The Casa Azul was a low, U-shaped building with a flat roof. Each room looked out onto a central courtyard. Frida moved back to her childhood home after she was married. The Casa Azul is now a beautiful museum dedicated to Frida's life and art. Visitors can see her studio and the bedroom where she painted during her long illness. The Casa Azul is still filled with Frida's possessions, her letters, and her large collection of Mexican art and objects.

This was Frida's home in Mexico, known as Casa Azul.

Developing Skills

After her accident, Frida did not return to school. She stayed at home, strapped to splints and bound by braces. Confined to bed, she began to paint. Her father lent her a box of oil paints. So Frida could paint in bed, her mother had a special easel built. She also had a mirrored canopy put up over Frida's bed so Frida could use herself as a model. The first subjects of Frida's paintings were her friends, her family, and herself.

When her health improved, Frida showed her paintings to the famous Mexican painter Diego Rivera. Frida had met Diego when he was painting murals at her school. Diego especially liked Frida's self-portraits and encouraged her to continue painting. The two artists became good friends. In 1929, when Frida was twenty-two and Diego forty-three, they married. They were one of the most talked-about couples in Mexico.

Early in their marriage, Frida traveled frequently with Diego to the United States. While spending time in other countries, Frida realized how proud she was of being Mexican. The history and culture of Mexico became an inspiration for Frida's art. She began to wear traditional Mexican clothing. In American cities, Frida stood out in her colorful skirts, shawls, and jewelry.

Although Frida and Diego divorced, they remarried several months later.

Frida captured many of the events of her life in her paintings. She also expressed her feelings of pain and sadness. She had thirty operations to repair her spine and her right foot, but Frida suffered from pain caused by the bus accident all her life.

Frida became pregnant several times, but her pregnancies were never successful. When she learned she would not be able to have children, she was heartbroken. Frida also struggled in her marriage. Diego was a difficult husband. At one point, she and Diego divorced. They remarried a short time later because they could not live apart from each other.

In spite of her emotional and physical suffering, Frida was a lively person. She had a wonderful sense of humor and a love for the dramatic. She surrounded herself with friends and festivity. Frida's witty and colorful paintings reflect her playfulness and her love of life.

"Painting completes my life. I lost three children and another series of things that would have filled my horrible life.... Painting is a substitute for all that. I think work is the best thing."

In 1931, Frida painted a mural for the San Francisco Stock Exchange. This is a portrait of a San Francisco society woman.

Frida with the Trotskys and Max Schachtman (far right), leader of the American Communist Committee.

Accomplishments

Many of Frida's paintings contain political themes. As a young woman, she joined the Young Communist League in Mexico City. She participated in many political marches and protests on behalf of the communist movement. In communism, she saw a political system that reflected her personal beliefs. In 1937, the Russian communist leader Leon Trotsky came to live in Mexico. Frida and Diego welcomed Trotsky and his wife with open arms. The Trotskys lived in Frida and Diego's home for two years, and Frida and Trotsky became close friends.

In 1938, Frida held her first **solo** show, in New York City. Audiences loved her work. After the New York show, Frida was no longer an amateur painter, but a professional artist. The next year, she traveled to Paris. The famous French artist André Breton had included several of Frida's paintings in his exhibit called "Mexique." Well-known artists of the day, such as Pablo Picasso and Marcel Duchamp, praised Frida's art.

"I really don't know if my paintings are surrealistic or not, but I do know that they are the most honest expression of myself."

Frida also taught art classes. At the National School of Painting and Sculpture, she encouraged her young students to draw the places and people around them. She took her students to paint their own neighborhoods, markets, and churches. When Frida became too ill to go to the school, she continued teaching from her bed at home. A group of her devoted students were named "Los Fridos" after their beloved teacher.

The first major **exhibition** of Frida's work in Mexico occurred several months before she died. Though she was confined to her bed and her doctors forbade her to move, she had no intention of missing the opening of her show. That night, she arrived at the gallery in an ambulance and was carried to a four-poster bed. From it, she greeted guests and sang Mexican ballads with her many friends.

Frida died just after her forty-seventh birthday in the Casa Azul, the house where she was born and where she painted. In 1984, the Mexican government declared her work part of the national heritage of Mexico.

Quick Notes

- **Frida painted more than fifty-five self-portraits. Each one showed what was happening in her life at that particular time.**

- **Frida's brilliant traditional Mexican clothing inspired fashion designers in New York City and Paris.**

- **Frida was involved in the international peace movement.**

- **Frida painted on many different surfaces, including tin, wood, and canvas.**

- **Frida loved animals and had many pets. At different times, she had dogs, cats, monkeys, birds, and even a deer.**

Frida often decorated her hair with colorful wool or flowers.

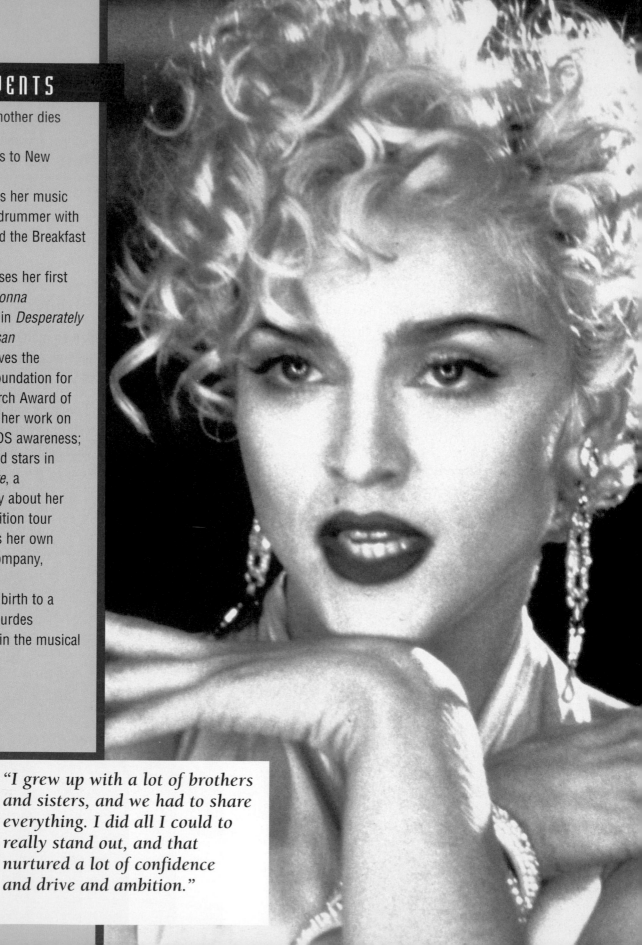

"I grew up with a lot of brothers and sisters, and we had to share everything. I did all I could to really stand out, and that nurtured a lot of confidence and drive and ambition."

Madonna

American Singer, Dancer, and Actor

Early Years

Madonna Louise Veronica Ciccone grew up in a large family in the suburbs of Detroit, Michigan. When Madonna was just five years old, her mother died of breast cancer. When her father remarried three years later, Madonna found it hard to accept her new stepmother.

The Ciccone children were encouraged to do well at school. For every A they received, their father paid them a quarter. Highly competitive, Madonna responded to the challenge and did exceptionally well in her classes. At school, Madonna showed her strong sense of independence. She arrived in uniform but would duck into the locker room to put on colorful socks and tie unusual bows in her hair.

All of the Ciccone children took music lessons. Madonna disliked piano and often hid instead of going to lessons. She finally convinced her father to enroll her in dance classes—ballet, jazz, tap, and baton. Madonna was a talented dancer and dreamed of becoming a star.

BACKGROUNDER

Mother and Daughter

The loss of her mother affected Madonna deeply. When her mother became sick with breast cancer, young Madonna did not understand the seriousness of her mother's illness. When her mother died, Madonna did not have the chance to say goodbye. Madonna knows very little about her mother, except that she was musical and loved to dance. Madonna singles out her mother's death as one of the most important events in her life. She has explored the loss of her mother in many of her songs.

Madonna's nickname when she was young was Nonni.

Developing Skills

When she graduated from high school, Madonna won a full scholarship to the University of Michigan's dance program. Madonna stayed at university for a year and a half. Then, with nothing but a suitcase full of dance clothes, a picture of her mother, and less than a hundred dollars, she moved to New York City. She was determined to be a star.

Madonna's break into show business did not happen overnight. She started out as a student with a well-known modern dance troupe. Frustrated with limited opportunities as a dancer, she soon quit the company. Madonna picked up a variety of odd jobs, working as a doughnut-shop waitress, a hat-check girl, and an artist's model. For several years, she lived in poverty, sleeping in cockroach-infested apartments and surviving on popcorn.

Madonna in 1982.

Madonna switched her focus from dance to music. She joined a group of musicians, learned to play guitar, and sang backup vocals. One of her first music jobs was as a drummer for a group called the Breakfast Club. Then, with a friend from Michigan, she formed a band and started writing and singing her own songs. Madonna recorded her pieces, sent the tape to record companies, and took it to the most popular dance clubs in New York. Eventually, the music industry noticed her.

In 1983, Madonna recorded her first album. After a slow start, two songs from the album made the top twenty on the popular music charts. Madonna quickly realized the importance of music videos in attracting fans. Madonna's first videos were filled with sensual dancing and appealing music. Her unique costumes launched a new look in fashion that was copied by teenage girls across the United States. Her later videos, which were even more daring, thrilled her fans and shocked her critics.

With her music career on the rise, Madonna also became a film actor. In 1985, she made her first widely released movie, *Desperately Seeking Susan.* As Susan, she played a creative, free-spirited woman, much like herself. Madonna showed that she could successfully perform a dramatic film role.

"The way I dressed in the beginning of my career was a reflection of me being incredibly poor.... Then, suddenly, that became the look, which was funny because I was just making the best of my situation."

BACKGROUNDER
Music Videos

In the past, many musical artists used film and television to promote their work. In 1981, Music TeleVision (MTV) began showing music videos across North America, twenty-four hours a day, every day of the week. Since then, music videos have become an important way to sell popular music. Music videos have also become a new form of popular art. Madonna was one of the first pop singers to use music videos to sell her records.

Madonna in Desperately Seeking Susan.

Quick Notes

- In high school, Madonna started a drama club. She played the lead roles in all its productions, including *My Fair Lady* and *The Sound of Music*.

- In 1990, the business magazine *Forbes* featured Madonna on its cover as America's top businesswoman of the year.

- In 1991, *Ladies' Home Journal* named Madonna one of the ten most powerful women in the United States.

- Madonna traveled to Argentina to research her role in the movie *Evita*.

- Madonna acted on Broadway in 1988 in the play *Speed the Plow*.

- Madonna had her Los Angeles mansion painted in red and yellow stripes.

Accomplishments

Since the mid-1980s, Madonna has become one of the most successful performing artists in the world. In 1990, her albums earned the Time Warner recording company more than five hundred million dollars.

Madonna is also a smart businesswoman. In 1992, she formed her own recording company called Maverick. Today, Maverick is a multimillion dollar business and a major player in the music industry. With a small group of trusted partners, Madonna manages Maverick. She is the main decision maker and takes an active role in all aspects of the company. Of her position at Maverick she says, "I do what I want. I'm the boss."

Madonna manages her own career with impressive focus and energy. She is an organized person with clear goals and high standards. Her busy work schedule, which includes a daily two-and-a-half hour workout, shows a high degree of self-discipline and ambition.

In 1996, Madonna arrives for the screening of her movie Evita.

Although her own life is very busy, Madonna is also interested in social issues. She has been a highly visible spokesperson on behalf of the **AIDS** awareness movement. Her interest is based on personal experience. Her first dance teacher and **mentor** died of AIDS, as have several other of Madonna's friends and colleagues. One of her world tours raised ten million dollars for AIDS research. In her 1989 album, *Like a Prayer*, she included an information sheet about AIDS prevention.

In much of her work, Madonna pokes fun at stereotypes, traditions, and attitudes in ways that some people find shocking. She believes in free expression and refuses to be silenced, even in the face of criticism.

Madonna has developed her career as a film actor. She has acted in sixteen movies. Playing the lead role in the musical film *Evita* was important to Madonna. She spent years learning about Eva Perón, the famous wife of Argentinian president Juan Perón. The film allowed her to develop her acting talent and reach a new audience.

Madonna's career has made a powerful impact on popular culture. She is a highly successful performing artist, a wealthy superstar, and a successful businesswoman.

> "I know that I'm not the best singer and I know I'm not the best dancer. But I'm not interested in that. I'm interested in pushing people's buttons and being provocative and being political."

BACKGROUNDER

Madonna and Censorship

Madonna's 1990 *Blonde Ambition* tour had considerable opposition. In Italy, some people objected to the show's portrayal of the Catholic Church. In Canada, the Toronto police threatened to arrest her if she did not change parts of her show. Madonna refused to bow to pressure. In the face of these challenges, she spoke out about her right to freedom of artistic expression.

Madonna received an Artist Achievement Award at the Billboard Music Awards in 1996.

Key Events

1953 Starts ballet lessons at the Vaganova School in Leningrad

1959 Joins the Kirov Ballet Company

1965 Wins a gold medal at the International Ballet Competition in Varna, Bulgaria

1970 Leaves the Soviet Union

1970–72 Dances with the American Ballet Theater in New York City

1974 Joins the Royal Ballet Company in London as a permanent guest artist

1978 Gives birth to a son, André

1980 Publishes her book, *A Dance Autobiography*

1983 Debuts on the Broadway stage in the popular musical *On Your Toes;* wins a Tony award

1989 Dances with the Kirov Ballet in her hometown, now known as St. Petersburg

1991 Begins a new career in dramatic acting

"I remember two things that had taken shape in me even as a child: curiosity and perfectionism."

Natalia Makarova

Russian Dancer

Early Years

Natalia Makarova was only six months old when World War II broke out in the Soviet Union and ended her family's quiet life in the city of Leningrad, now known as St. Petersburg. Natalia was sent to live with her grandmother in a small village far from the city. When the war was over and Natalia was five years old, she returned to Leningrad. Life was difficult, and no one had enough to eat. Natalia lived with her mother and her stepfather in an apartment they shared with several families.

At school, Natalia worked hard and earned good grades. She was a loner, with a quick temper that often got her into trouble. At home, she did not feel part of her mother's new family, which now included a baby brother.

Natalia began dancing by accident. When she was twelve, she went with her friends to sign up for gymnastics at the communist youth organization. On a whim, she joined the ballet club instead. Natalia felt awkward next to the other dancers, like "an ugly duckling among swans." After each class, she went home in tears, but the challenge excited her, and she was determined to continue.

BACKGROUNDER

The Effects of War in Leningrad

In 1939, at the beginning of World War II, the Soviet Union and Germany were allies, promising not to invade each other's country. In June 1941, the German army made a surprise attack against the Soviet Union. By the winter, the Germans had surrounded Leningrad. They destroyed much of the city, and many soldiers and civilians lost their lives. During and after the war, the citizens of Leningrad struggled to survive. The city's buildings and economy were in ruins.

BACKGROUNDER
The Kirov Ballet

The Vaganova School was the largest ballet school in Europe. Young dancers from the Soviet Union and Eastern Europe went there to study classical ballet. After nine years of intense training, the best dancers joined the Kirov Ballet, one of the Soviet Union's two major ballet companies. The Kirov, famous for its tradition of classical ballet, has been a home to some of the best dancers in the world.

Natalia dancing in the ballet Swan Lake.

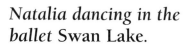

Developing Skills

Again on an impulse, and without telling her parents, Natalia applied to the Vaganova School of Ballet. At thirteen, she was older than most first-year Vaganova students. She was part of a special program that prepared dancers in just six years. Natalia had a great deal to learn. Every day, Natalia took two hours of ballet lessons. In addition to her regular academic classes, she studied the history of ballet, music, and art. She learned to play the piano and to speak and read French.

After six years of study and hard work, Natalia was ready to graduate from the Vaganova School and become a dancer in the Kirov Ballet Company. For her final exam, she performed a dance from the classic ballet *Giselle*. The critics were impressed.

Natalia quickly rose through the ranks of the Kirov Ballet to become a **principal** dancer. Soon, she was recognized as a brilliant new star. Ballet dancers were held in high esteem in the Soviet Union. Natalia earned a very good salary. She had her own apartment, and unlike most Soviet citizens, was allowed to travel to other countries.

During her years at the Kirov Ballet, Natalia danced many of the great roles in classical ballet. Gradually, she became frustrated with dancing only the same traditional pieces. She was an imaginative person who wanted to experiment with her art. During her travels, Natalia had seen the types of dance being performed in the West. She wanted to dance in these new, challenging ballets. The Soviet government, however, did not allow this kind of artistic freedom. It tightly controlled the type of art being produced.

In 1970, Natalia was on tour with the Kirov Ballet in London, England. One evening, she met some English friends for dinner. They began to discuss the differences between ballet in the Soviet Union and other countries. Quite suddenly, Natalia decided she wanted to **defect** from the Soviet Union and move to England. That night, Natalia left behind her whole world, including her family, her friends, and her country.

"I have a carefree nature. I can say good-bye to the past without difficulty and never go back to it."

The Soviet government immediately removed her many honors and awards. Her name was erased from her country's official records, including all ballet books and encyclopedias. It was as if she had never existed. It would be nineteen years before Natalia would be allowed to return to her homeland.

In 1970, Natalia had her New York City debut with the American Ballet Theater.

Quick Notes

- After Natalia's defection, the Soviet government refused to allow Natalia's mother to travel to other countries.

- In 1980, Natalia published her book, *A Dance Autobiography,* about her life as a dancer.

- In the early 1990s, Natalia narrated three recordings for children that combine favorite traditional stories and classical music.

- In 1991, Natalia starred in the London production of the play *Tovarich.*

- Natalia still keeps fit by exercising for one and a half hours each day. She also enjoys reading plays and going to the theater.

Natalia and Rudolf Nureyev rehearse for a performance of Swan Lake.

Accomplishments

Natalia had to rebuild her career from scratch. She had many loyal fans, but no company with which to dance. During the first year of her exile, she performed in two televised ballets with her fellow Russian **émigré**, the dancer Rudolf Nureyev. That same year, Natalia moved to New York City to perform with the American Ballet Theater.

Her time in New York was difficult. Natalia could not speak English very well, and she was overwhelmed by the practical details of life. She was lonely and missed her mother. To cope, Natalia buried herself in work, rehearsing eight hours a day and performing at night. She learned new roles and new styles of dance, including jazz.

Natalia left the American Ballet Theater after two years. She then performed on many of the world's most famous stages, in Italy, Sweden, Germany, France, and South Africa. In 1974, she returned to London and joined the Royal Ballet as a permanent guest artist. Always exploring new dance techniques, Natalia successfully experimented with acting on the Broadway stage. Her 1983 performance in the musical *On Your Toes* earned her a Tony award.

Since Natalia's departure from the Soviet Union in 1970, the Kirov Ballet had not returned to London. In the late 1980s, a new mood of freedom and openness was changing life in the Soviet Union. In 1988, the Kirov Ballet went to London and invited Natalia to dance with them. Natalia performed to sell-out crowds. Several months later, Natalia made an emotional return to her homeland and danced at the Kirov Theater. Seated in the audience was her mother. Although Natalia and her mother had spoken regularly on the telephone, they had not seen each other for nearly twenty years.

Natalia hung up her ballet shoes after her performances at the Kirov. Even in her retirement, she has not left the stage far behind. In 1989, she made the documentary film *Ballerina* describing the dancer's art. Recently, she has focused on developing her acting career.

"*Everything I have achieved came through my own accomplishments. Nobody helped me.... Basically I had to fight for what I got.*"

BACKGROUNDER
Glasnost and Perestroika

In the 1980s, Soviet leader Mikhail Gorbachev introduced new policies that changed life in the Soviet Union. *Glasnost* (openness) and *perestroika* (restructuring) ended some of the tight government controls on the Soviet economy and society. Elections were held, and people were allowed greater freedom in many aspects of their lives. The government slowly welcomed back citizens who had defected.

Natalia rehearses with the Kirov Ballet in 1988— eighteen years after she defected during the company's visit to London.

"Where and how I have lived is unimportant. It is what I have done with where I have been that should be of interest."

Georgia O'Keeffe

American Artist

Early Years

Georgia O'Keeffe grew up on a large dairy farm outside Sun Prairie, Wisconsin. As one of seven children in a house filled with grandparents, aunts, and uncles, Georgia preferred to be on her own. She loved to walk in the fields with her father or sneak away and quietly play with her dolls.

Even as a child, Georgia noticed and remembered small details. As an adult, she could remember the patterns of sunlight and shadows on a quilt she lay on as a baby. Like all her sisters, Georgia took private art lessons, first at home, then traveling to town by buggy. Her teacher asked her to copy pictures, but outside of class, Georgia worked on her own creations, experimenting with color and light.

When Georgia was twelve, she announced that she was going to be an artist. It was an unusual choice. Georgia had never met a professional artist, nor had she seen much art. In those days, art was considered a hobby for women, not a career. Georgia's mother recognized her daughter's talent and encouraged her to pursue her goal.

BACKGROUNDER

Women in the Visual Arts

When Georgia was growing up, girls were not encouraged to take up art seriously. Creating was something women did for fun in their spare time. They quilted, wove baskets, made pottery, or sketched, but their art was not thought important enough to display in museums. Women were just starting to be allowed to go to professional art schools. A few became art teachers, but none became professional artists.

Georgia's art was appreciated by many. She is seen here with a prominent art collector.

Developing Skills

At times, Georgia was frustrated with teachers who tried to control her work by telling her exactly how her pictures should look. When the O'Keeffe family moved to Virginia, she continued to take art classes. One of her teachers recognized Georgia's talent and encouraged her. Georgia was chosen to be the art editor of her school's yearbook. Her watercolor of red and yellow corn won the school art prize.

In 1907, Georgia began her training as a professional artist at the Art Institute of Chicago. Although the family was struggling to get along, her mother had scraped together the money for Georgia's fees. Two years later, Georgia went to New York City to attend the Art Students League, a popular art school. After a year, she was forced to give up her studies when her family could no longer afford to pay her tuition. She moved back to Chicago to work in advertising, churning out drawings for clothing ads. Exhausted from her work, Georgia had no time for her own painting. When she became seriously ill with measles, she went back home to Virginia. When she was well, she slowly returned to painting.

At a summer art class, Georgia discovered a new kind of art. Until then, she had been painting in a realistic way, sketching models and copying the style of other artists. Georgia wanted to find her own style and began to experiment with **abstraction**. She learned new ways to use line, space, and shape in designs from her own imagination. She discovered that "art could be a thing of your own."

"I found I could say things with color and shapes that I couldn't say in any other way—things I had no words for."

Over the next few years, Georgia began to develop a new style. She taught art in South Carolina, and she used her free time to experiment with her own work. She shut herself up alone in her studio and put her paints away. Expressing her own ideas and feelings, she created simple charcoal drawings in black and white. For the first time, she was drawing only to please herself.

Georgia sent some of her new work to a friend in New York City on the condition that she not show it to anyone. Georgia's friend was so impressed with these new drawings, she could not keep them to herself. She took them to the famous photographer and artist Alfred Stieglitz. When Georgia discovered that Alfred was showing the drawings in his gallery, she was enraged and demanded that he remove them. Alfred told Georgia that her drawings were wonderful and convinced her to let them stay. Their stormy first meeting resulted in a professional partnership and later, marriage.

BACKGROUNDER
The New York Art Scene

In the early part of the century, New York City was an exciting place for young artists. The city was filled with new ideas about art. With his gallery and his reputation as a photographer, Alfred Stieglitz was at the center of this world. He introduced Americans to the works of Picasso, Cézanne, and other famous artists. Alfred also encouraged many young American painters.

Georgia with her husband, Alfred Stieglitz.

Quick Notes

- For many years, Georgia lived with very little money. She could not afford to buy clothes, so she learned to sew her own. She found sewing a way to relax.

- After Alfred died, Georgia traveled throughout the world to Europe, South America, India, Asia, and Egypt.

- In 1997, the Georgia O'Keeffe Museum opened in Santa Fe, New Mexico. More than 250,000 people visited the museum in its first year.

- As Georgia grew older, she led a very private life, but she was still involved in the life of her New Mexican village. She bought baseball uniforms for the village team and gave money to other community projects.

- The two-hundred-year old **adobe** house in Abiquiu where Georgia lived and worked in New Mexico is now a national historic site.

Accomplishments

Alfred continued to show Georgia's work in his gallery. Almost immediately, the public liked and paid good prices for her paintings. When Georgia moved to Texas to be head of an art school, she kept in touch with Alfred. She returned to New York City, and eventually, she and Alfred were married. They were two of the best-known artists in the city. Strikingly dressed in black, the couple were part of the city's exciting modern art scene.

Georgia's artistic inspiration, however, came mainly from the countryside. Each summer, she and Alfred traveled to his family's property in upstate New York. Georgia especially loved to paint flowers. For her, they seemed to contain the beauty of life. Georgia painted huge flowers, up close and in intense colors. She said, "I will make even busy New Yorkers take time to see what I see of flowers."

"I'll paint what I see—what the flower is to me, but I'll paint it big and they will be surprised into taking time to look at it."

Georgia with her painting entitled "Life and Death."

Georgia developed a distinctive style. She was a strong, independent woman who painted from her own point of view. She was irritated by critics who called her a woman painter. Georgia believed she was simply a painter with no need for other labels.

Over the years, Georgia became increasingly unhappy living in New York. In 1929, she visited New Mexico with a friend and fell in love with the desert. For the next few years, Georgia returned each summer to New Mexico. She finally bought a house near the artist community of Taos, high in the mountains. When Alfred died of a heart attack in 1946, Georgia moved to New Mexico permanently.

Over time, Georgia's eyesight began to fail. She hung huge canvases in her garage so she could continue to paint. When she could no longer see, she created sculptures. Georgia died when she was ninety-eight years old.

Throughout her long career, Georgia created over nine-hundred works, many of which have been shown in major art museums. She rarely signed her work, but her paintings need no signature. They have become some of the best-known images of our time.

Georgia's love for the Southwest was obvious in her style of dress, as well as in her art.

BACKGROUNDER
O'Keeffe and the American Southwest

As a child, Georgia loved the stories her mother read aloud about the Wild West. When she first visited Texas, Georgia was overwhelmed. "This was my country," she said. "Terrible winds and a wonderful emptiness." Several years later, she spent a summer in New Mexico. She fell in love with the light, the sky, and the desert landscapes. Even though she had to return to New York City that fall, she wanted to keep working on her desert paintings. She packed up a barrel of animal bones to bring with her. Georgia called these bones "my symbols of the desert." Georgia's New Mexico paintings soon became as famous as her flower paintings.

KEY EVENTS

1963 Graduates with an undergraduate degree in philosophy, fine art, and education

1964 Records her first album, *It's My Way;* named *Billboard* magazine's "Best New Artist"

1967 Moves to Hawaii

1976 Gives birth to her son, Dakota; joins the cast of *Sesame Street*

1982 Wins an Academy Award for "Up Where We Belong," the theme song for the film *An Officer and a Gentleman*

1984 Starts creating visual art using the computer

1993 France names Buffy Best International Artist of the year

1995 Inducted into the Canadian Music Hall of Fame

1996 Wins First Americans in the Arts Award for Lifetime Musical Achievement; starts the Cradleboard Teaching Project

1998 Named an officer in the Order of Canada

"The real Art occurs in the imagination: then the Work begins. The tools are whatever we can get, beads or pixels, hunting bows or a computer."

Buffy Sainte-Marie

Canadian Singer, Songwriter, Actor, and Artist

Early Years

Beverly Sainte-Marie was born on a Cree reserve in western Canada. Orphaned as a baby, she was adopted by a part-Mi'kmaq couple. They raised their young daughter, nicknamed Buffy, in a small town in Maine.

A shy, thoughtful child, Buffy enjoyed wandering the woods near her home. When she was four, she taught herself to play the family piano. As she grew older, Buffy started composing songs, setting her own words to music. Her songs told about what was happening in her life, both the happy things and the sad things.

When Buffy was a teenager, her father gave her a second-hand guitar. She taught herself to play the guitar in her own style. As an adult, she still plays the guitar in her own unique way. Buffy also learned to play the mouth bow, an unusual Native-American instrument.

BACKGROUNDER

Native Reserves

Hundreds of thousands of native people in Canada and the United States live on reserves. Native peoples "reserved" these lands for their own use, while giving up most of their lands to the government. On many reserves, the native way of life continues. There, people speak their own language, practise their own spiritual beliefs, and share traditional values. Many native people see their reserves as a spiritual and cultural home.

Buffy's connection to her heritage has been an inspiration since she started writing music.

Developing Skills

W hen Buffy started classes at the University of Massachusetts, she wanted to become a veterinarian. Soon, she decided she was too "tender-hearted" to be a vet. She studied oriental philosophy, fine art, and education instead. Buffy continued to play guitar and sing at college. Friends encouraged her to perform at local coffeehouses, and Buffy soon became a popular folk singer on campus. When she graduated, Buffy was named one of the ten most outstanding members of her class. She was planning to be an elementary school teacher.

Buffy retreated to Maine to decide whether or not she wanted to pursue a career as a folk singer.

In 1963, Buffy visited New York City. Guitar in hand, she got up to sing at a coffeehouse in Greenwich Village, an area of New York City known for its music and art. The folk music critic from *The New York Times* happened to be in the audience and saw Buffy perform. In his newspaper column, he called her one of the most promising new talents in folk music. Buffy appeared at several other small **venues** in Greenwich Village. She was soon receiving offers to do concerts and make records. As Buffy remembers, "I became a professional singer and songwriter by accident ... I never expected to last more than a year or two."

In 1964, a year after her college graduation, Buffy recorded her first album. Each year for seven years, she released a new album, and each one was a bestseller. Buffy became a popular folk artist in North America and in other countries.

Buffy found a receptive audience. She sang about love and about war and injustice. In the 1960s, many people were questioning some of the values and assumptions of the past and speaking out against war. In her song "Universal Soldier" Buffy wrote that individuals must take responsibility for war. "Universal Soldier" became an anthem for those people who opposed American involvement in the Vietnam War.

Early in her music career, Buffy drew attention to the experience of native people in North America. Many of her songs tell about native culture and the importance of rights for native peoples. As she toured the world with her music, Buffy loved visiting nearby native communities. She became a popular lecturer working to correct society's **stereotypes** of native people.

"If I stand for anything, it should be called Indian rights, pacifism and alternative thinking."

BACKGROUNDER
The Vietnam War

In the 1960s, the United States became involved in the war between North and South Vietnam in Southeast Asia. By 1969, nearly 550,000 American troops had been sent to fight against the communist North Vietnamese and their supporters in the South, the Viet Cong. In the United States, many Americans opposed the war. Large demonstrations were held in major cities and on college campuses. Protesters urged the government to get out of the war. Hundreds of thousands of people died during the war. By the end of fighting in 1972, casualties included 50,000 Americans, 400,000 South Vietnamese, and over 900,000 North Vietnamese and Viet Cong.

Buffy holds a Ph.D. in fine art, in addition to her degrees in Oriental philosophy and teaching.

Accomplishments

By 1969, Buffy had written over two hundred songs. Well-known singers, such as Elvis Presley and Barbra Streisand, sang her songs and made them famous. In the mid-1970s, Buffy retired from her busy music career to raise her son in Hawaii. Even during her retirement, Buffy stayed in the public eye. She and her son, Dakota, joined the cast of the popular children's program *Sesame Street* for five years. On *Sesame Street*, she appeared as herself. Buffy wanted her young audience "to know one thing above all: that Indians exist. We are not all dead and stuffed in museums like the dinosaurs."

Today, Buffy continues her work in native awareness and education. She writes articles on native life for several publications and is associated with three universities. In 1996, she established the Cradleboard Teaching Project. Through it, Buffy provides students and teachers with learning materials on native culture. She also gives native and non-native children a way to communicate by computer so they can get to know more about one another.

In native communities, Buffy is a powerful role model. Young people on reserves in the United States and Canada sing her songs and are proud of her fame. The editor of a native magazine has said that Buffy is "like our Elvis." As a supporter of native artists, Buffy helped establish an award for native music in Canada. The organization First Americans in the Arts named its award for lifetime musical achievement after Buffy.

For many years, Buffy has used the computer to compose music for movies and for her own songs. She used it to record her 1991 album *Coincidence and Likely Stories*. In the early 1980s, she started using her computer to create visual art. Buffy says "painting on a computer monitor screen is literally painting with light." She has had several exhibitions of her works, many of which have sold in Europe and Canada. Buffy also teaches digital art in her position as artist-in-residence at a native arts institute in New Mexico.

Buffy uses her art and her music to share her strong beliefs in human rights and a just society. As a prominent Native American, she works to improve her people's future. Buffy says, "I do a lot of what I want. I'm not in the rat race of show business."

This is a self-portrait that Buffy created using her electronic painting technique.

Quick Notes

- **Buffy has personally funded many scholarships for native students to attend college.**

- **Buffy has also worked as an actor. In 1968, she appeared in an episode of the television series *The Virginian*. She insisted that all native roles in the episode be played by native people. In 1994, Buffy acted in the television movie *The Broken Chain*.**

- **Elvis Presley made Buffy's song "Until It's Time for You To Go" a big hit. Buffy used the money she earned from Presley's recording to help pay for her projects as an educator.**

- **Buffy exhibits her digital paintings at art galleries and in museums. Buffy's home page contains several examples of her digital paintings and a description of how she creates them.**

More Women in Profile

The following pages list a few more women performers and visual artists you may want to read about on your own. Use the Suggested Reading list to learn about these and other women in the visual and performing arts.

Debbie Allen

1950–

Debbie Allen

American Dancer, Choreographer, and Actor

Debbie started dancing when she was three years old. As an African American, Debbie faced racism in her dance career. As a result, she studied theater and speech at college. In 1980, she took a lead in the Broadway musical *West Side Story*. A small part as a dance teacher in the movie *Fame* landed Debbie a leading role in the popular television series of the same name. For five years, Debbie acted in the show, **choreographed** many dance routines, and directed several episodes.

1915–1982

Ingrid Bergman

Swedish Actor

Ingrid acted in several films in Sweden before she became a Hollywood star. Since childhood, she had wanted a career in the theater. Ingrid overcame her shyness as a teenager and attended theater school in Stockholm. A few years later, an American agent spotted her performance in the Swedish film *Intermezzo*. The American version of the film was a box-office hit and launched Ingrid's Hollywood career. One of her last performances before she died of breast cancer was an award-winning television movie about the life of Israeli Prime Minister Golda Meir.

1871–1945

Emily Carr

Canadian Artist

Emily's paintings of the Canadian landscape have become some of the best-known works of Canadian art. In her early years, Emily struggled to make a living as a painter, and many years passed before her work was appreciated. Emily visited and painted native villages and the coastal forests and beaches on the west coast of Canada. When in her sixties and no longer able to paint, Emily wrote several best-selling books about her life and travels.

1907–1994

Devika Rani Chaudhurry

Indian Actor

In the 1930s, Devika was one of the most famous movie stars in India. Early in her career, Devika studied drama, music, and architecture in London, England. A successful fabric designer, she started out in film behind the scenes designing costumes. In 1934, Devika and her husband, Himansu Rai, started their own movie studio in India. Devika became the star of the Bombay Talkies studio. When her husband died, Devika managed the company on her own.

1919–1991

Margot Fonteyn

British Dancer

Peggy Hookham began her long career as Britain's prima ballerina when she was fourteen. Using the stage name Margot Fonteyn, she danced with the Royal Ballet for her entire career. Many ballets were created especially for her. In 1962, when she was forty-three, Margot danced with Rudolf Nureyev, the famous Russian **émigré** who was almost twenty years younger than she. Soon, Fonteyn and Nureyev were the most exciting ballet duo in the world. Because of the physical demands of a dance career, many dancers retire in their late thirties or forties. Margot danced until she was fifty-seven.

1886–1988

Clementine Hunter

American Artist

Clementine lived a hard life on a Louisiana cotton plantation. She was in her early fifties when she tried painting. Her employer gave her some used tubes of oil paints, and Clementine started to experiment. She painted her first picture on an old windowshade. Later, she painted on whatever she could find: paper bags, empty bottles, and cardboard boxes. Clementine painted stories from the Bible and scenes from her memory of daily life on the plantation. Her friends bought her pictures, and soon museums were clamoring to buy them, too. Clementine stopped painting just one month before she died at 101 years old.

Clementine Hunter

1949–

Annie Leibovitz

American Photographer

Annie got her first camera during a trip to Japan when she was a student at the San Francisco Art Institute. When she returned to school, she immediately signed up for a photography class. In 1970, Annie was hired by a new rock music magazine called *Rolling Stone*. Soon, she became the magazine's chief photographer. Annie was known for her **candid**, daring, and witty pictures of some of the most famous music stars in the world. By getting to know her subjects, she was able to make them relax in front of the camera and try unusual poses. Since leaving *Rolling Stone* in the early 1980s, Annie has worked as chief photographer at *Vanity Fair* magazine.

1915–1963

Edith Piaf

French Singer, Songwriter, and Actor

Edith Gassion had a difficult childhood. She was orphaned at an early age. Meningitis, a disease affecting the brain, caused young Edith to lose her eyesight for several years. She started her career singing in the streets of Paris, France. Soon, she moved her act to music halls and nightclubs. A small woman, Edith was nicknamed "Piaf" after the Parisian slang for little sparrow.

Edith became famous throughout Europe and North America for her expressive voice and the sad songs she wrote about life on the street.

1930–

Faith Ringgold

American Artist

Faith had always wanted to be an artist, but women were not allowed to study art at the nearby college. She became an art teacher in New York City instead. In her classes, she encouraged her students to use fabric and beads. One day, a student asked Faith why she did not use fabric and beads in her own work. The question caused Faith to start exploring. She began to make traditional cloth masks like those of her African ancestors. She also became a performance artist, accompanying many of her artworks with singing, dancing, and storytelling.

Edith Piaf

1942–
Barbra Streisand
American Singer, Actor, and Director

Barbra is one of the top-selling female recording artists of the twentieth century. She has recorded fifty titles and sold over fifty-two million albums in the United States. Barbra got her start as a performer singing in New York City nightclubs in the 1960s. The role of the entertainer Fanny Brice in the Broadway musical *Funny Girl* was her first major success. The movie version won Barbra an Academy Award. She has since starred in fifteen films, several of which she has written, directed, and produced. In 1994, Barbra returned to the concert stage after an absence of more than twenty years with two successful performances in Las Vegas.

1939–
Lily Tomlin
American Comedian and Actor

Lily's comedy career began with a role in a college variety show. In 1965, Lily moved to New York City to look for work as an actor. She found small jobs in television commercials and performed her comedy routines on television talk shows. In 1969, Lily joined the cast of the television show *Laugh-In*. Her characters, the telephone operator Ernestine and the little girl Edith Ann, won her many awards and many fans. Lily has acted in more than eleven films and created and performed a successful one-woman stage show that has toured North America. She returned to television to play a lead role in the series *Murphy Brown* and as the voice of Ms. Frizzle on the children's program *The Magic School Bus*.

1959–
Tracey Ullmann
British Singer and Actor

As a ten-year-old, Tracey was inspired to sing by a Liza Minnelli album she received as a gift. She started formal theatrical training when she was twelve at an Italian stage school. At sixteen, having been expelled from school, she found work as a chorus girl in Berlin, Germany. When Tracey returned to England, she landed a part in the stage production of *The Rocky Horror Picture Show*. In 1984, she released an album of songs that introduced her to American audiences. A few years later, Tracey starred in her own television series and in 1990, made her first film.

Tracey Ullmann

Glossary

abstraction: a style of painting that groups shapes and color in patterns rather than trying to imitate reality

adobe: sun-dried brick

AIDS: a disease that destroys the body's ability to fight disease and infection

apprenticeship: when someone is taught a trade or craft in exchange for low wages

candid: a photograph taken informally, without the subject's knowledge

choreograph: to plan the arrangement of dance steps for a performance

debut: the first public appearance of a performer on the stage

decade: a period of ten years

defect: to leave one's country illegally

duet: a musical piece for two instruments or voices

émigré: a person who has left his or her country to settle in another, usually for political reasons

exhibition: a collection of art arranged for people to look at

mentor: an experienced and trusted advisor

polio: a virus that attacks the brain and spinal cord

principal: main or leading performer

revue: a theatrical performance consisting of short songs and sketches

solo: something done without a companion or partner

stereotype: a conventional, overly simple opinion

venues: places for meetings, events, or concerts

Suggested Reading

Arntz, James, and Thomas S. Wilson. *Julie Andrews*. Chicago: Contemporary Books, 1995.

Bremser, Martha, ed. *International Dictionary of Ballet*. Detroit: St. James Press, 1993.

Hacker, Carlotta. *Great African Americans in the Arts*. Niagara-on-the-Lake: Crabtree Publishing, 1997.

King, Norman. *Madonna: The Book*. New York: William Morrow, 1991.

Makarova, Natalia. *A Dance Autobiography*. London: Adam and Charles Black, 1980.

Pickard, Roy. *The Oscar Stars From A–Z*. London: Headline Book Publishing, 1996.

Rajadhyaksha, Ashish, and Paul Willemen. *Encyclopedia of Indian Cinema*. London: British Film Institute Press, 1994.

Romanowski, Patricia, and Holly George-Warren, eds. *The New Rolling Stone Encyclopedia of Rock & Roll*. New York: Rolling Stone Press, 1995.

Sainte-Marie, Buffy. *Cradleboard Teaching Project*. Worldwide Web: www.cradleboard.org

Sills, Leslie. *Inspirations: Stories about Women Artists*. Niles, Illinois: Albert Whitman & Company, 1989.

Smith, Ronald L. *Who's Who in Comedy*. New York: Facts on File, 1992.

Turner, Robyn Montana. *Frida Kahlo*. Boston: Little, Brown and Company, 1993.

Turner, Robyn Montana. *Georgia O'Keeffe*. Boston: Little, Brown and Company, 1991.

Index

1 2 3 4 5 6 7 8 9 0 Printed in Canada 8 7 6 5 4 3 2 1 0 9